The Summer of Agios Dimitrios

Also by Peter Hughes:

The Interior Designer's Late Morning, Many Press 1983
Bar Magenta (with Simon Marsh), Many Press, 1986
Odes on St. Cecilia's Day, Poetical Histories, 1990
The Metro Poems, Many Press, 1992
Psyche in the Gargano, Equipage, 1995
Paul Klee's Diary, Equipage, 1995
Keith Tippet Plays Tonight, Maquette Press, 1999
Blueroads: Selected Poems, Salt Publishing, 2003
Sound Signals Advising of Presence, infernal methods, 2006
Nistanimera, Shearsman Books, 2007
The Sardine Tree, Oystercatcher Press, 2008

Peter Hughes

The Summer
of Agios Dimitrios

Shearsman Books
Exeter

First published in the United Kingdom in 2009 by
Shearsman Books Ltd
58 Velwell Road
Exeter EX4 4LD

www.shearsman.com

ISBN 978-1-84861-064-4
First edition

Copyright © Peter Hughes, 2009.

The right of Peter Hughes to be identified as the author of this work has been asserted by him in accordance with the Copyrights, Designs and Patents Act of 1988. All rights reserved.

Acknowledgements:
Some of these poems have appeared in *Beard of Bees, Exultations & Difficulties, Fragmente, Geometer, Numinous Magazine, Shadow Train, Stimulus Response, Tears in the Fence* and *Poetry Wales*.

Cover image: from a photograph taken inside the ruins of the Trissakia church by the author.

for Lynn

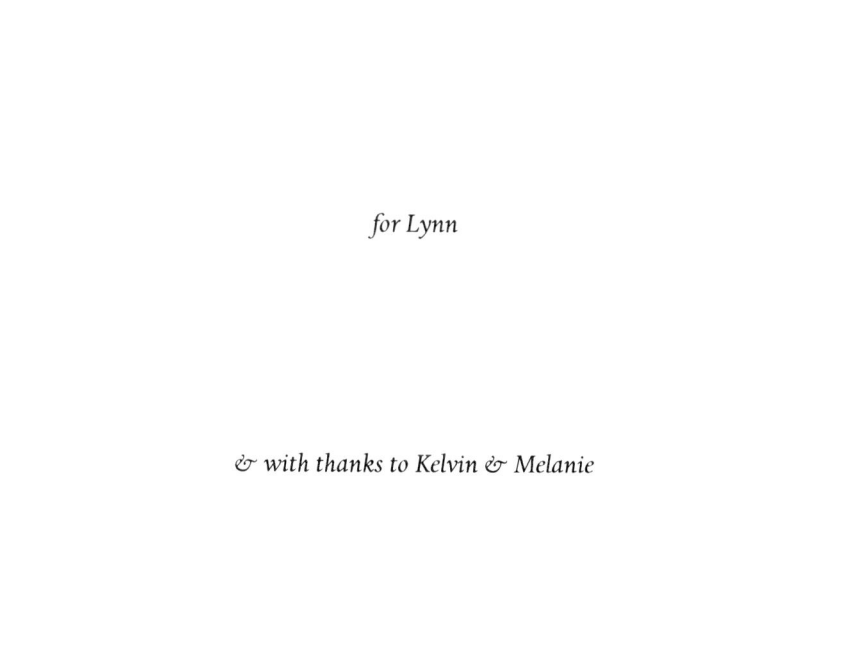

& with thanks to Kelvin & Melanie

The Summer of Agios Dimitrios

1.1 Wednesday 12th September

only after take-off
do you see a range of places
where you could have walked the dog
if only you'd had one
& those oddly-shaped bodies of water
which are never there when you get back
our heads in the clouds
& in the inner distance
we heard goat bells on wild promontories
the sea almost too bright to see
feral sea-nymphs nudging the rudders
of sailors who scratch their heads
under sea-stained caps
lick a finger & stick it in the sky
shrug
then put in for a bottle of Mythos
& a cheese pie
on the plank outside
in the sunny dust
peaches
bleached French beans
& a row of slightly deflated
weeping purple figs
at the height of their powers

1.2 Thursday 13th September

all-day breakfast all day
peer into unfamiliar
books & rock pools
end up eating a goat
stew reading up on local lore
disguised as a deer
to escape the lust of Zeus
she nevertheless
crumpled under violence
& the outcome of more rape
was a foul taste
called Sparta
she hanged herself
on this vast mountain
continuing
beyond the horizon
became a dove
then one of the Pleiades
it never says anywhere
she became a corpse
looking eastwards
from the village at night
you register the shape
of the mountain
by the absence of stars

1.3 Friday 14th September

the mountain top clear
of cloud I can hear
the sea under star
shapes above the eucalyptus
cicada plucking at
distance some say
Cygnus some Northern
Cross either way almost
lost in a fertile haze of milky
way a mosquito followed a
bat through the night & out
the other side to morning
shadow of the jasmine on
a bowl as I rinse out
the mop some say it's all
written but I'd fold it
again & again
until it fits my smallest
pocket & walk
into the water

1.4 Saturday 15th September

sun swallows behind
the violet rim of land
between sea & sky
an unfamiliar breeze
pecks the table
questioning our intentions & spelling
this page is held down
by the clips they use
to anchor tablecloths
in tavernas along the coast
the paper is sun-bright orange
then grey
now lit by an electric glare & almost dead
if you don't know how to spell a word
you can always use another
the garden hose doesn't reach
the bottle brush tree
so we carry it six bowls of water
then back away
as it exhales

1.5 Sunday 16th September

the speechless water
Ritsos carried in his hands
reappeared in Elytis
near the church of St John
on whose day in midsummer
a child fetches water
from the local spring or well
& carries it back without speaking
every child in the village
places a small belonging
into the water
which is then covered
with a red cloth
the container is left
outdoors all night
so the stars may move over it
come morning
the cloth is removed
& each child's possession
is restored
now poems on
the future of the children
can be made

1.6 Monday 17th September

three people are poised
on the church tower
in Nomitsi
each at a different level
they allow
some sky into the structure
the next church
has a miniature door
& two long curving palm leaves
as tall as a person
framing the entrance
but the finest is
the last church
the metamorphosis
in which you hear
still the builders' voices
at different levels
the great clarity of the air means
you can shout really loud
many local calls can be made
without a phone
inside the church
a little light came in from here
& there the wooden offertory plate
was filled with change

1.7 Tuesday 18th September

early morning darkness
thins over the mountain
Venus a hand high
above the ridge
moving up and away
lights still on in the village square
but in the garden it's light enough
to read your own writing
the sound of waves
close & gentle
two boats heading out
say south west
maybe five degrees apart
leave the village
faster than they
leave each other

2.1 Wednesday 19th September

boil Greek French beans & pour rough red wine
just room on the Belling for a tiny frying pan
to perch—a latecomer with one cheek parked on
a hard shared chair—next to the fat pot of steam
room in the pan for three sausages chopped in half
push the six into different positions with onion &
peppers like that Chinese game they never invented before
shunting sausages into a siding to fry courgettes
fry savagely but do not burn garlic chop tomatoes & add to
onion add ouzo heat & tip into bowl that came free with tuna
multi-pack which if spun round fast may sling out
a tin to catch the neighbour's cat that squirts
the geraniums on its hip (offside/rear) pour bean
water into pot for rice then mix everything together
& squirt with lemon juice to give the illusion of 'cookery'
serve with ¾ gallon of cold white wine neighbour
affably wonders why cat has one eyebrow raised & limp

2.2 Thursday 20th September

four in the morning sea stirring
on three sides of peninsula
Orion flat out on mountain top
too tired & hot to stay in bedroom
mosquitoes stretching skin of air
tight like haunted drum in stomach
outside in a large darkness cool air sets
with jasmine scent all over the skin
you have to sleep sometime
then transplant this tree into
a hole in the earth
a dog comes up for a look
stares in the hole
stares at me
stares back in the hole & sighs
lies down
goes back to sleep
upside down in the dust
another line is written & changed
before the clay sets

2.3 Friday 21st September

it's easy now to get back
where we were
the place so hard
to reach at the beginning
just follow the road
& catch drops of rain
each fat as a fig
sleep involved much waking up
from dreams fuelled
by brown white wine & brandy
I couldn't save you from being pushed
into a woodland pond by a happy
animal part lassie part lion that
balanced its paws on your shoulders
until you toppled into waking
it's better to know the truth
sit on the step
& write in gentle rain

2.4 Saturday 22nd September

the steep mule track
clambers up from Kotroni
past four builders pale with rock dust
cheese pies & milk
fetched by the youngest
on an orange moped
from down in the next village
there's a lot of wild sage
up to the dirt road that crosses your path
taking you along the contour line
deep into the wooded valley
there's a spring in a cave
a pink plastic cup
a magical crab
six hundred feet above sea level
whose oracular utterances
are conveyed by claw signals
& bee-like manoeuvring
left & right & fore & aft
drink it while you can
put the pink plastic
cup back & walk the line

2.5 Sunday 23rd September

cover the cupboard in wet blue paint
reinflate the punctured dinghy
adding a see-through superglue
scab on its hole
embark on an initial voyage
but neglect to placate Poseidon
who hisses underneath as we paddle
along the sharp Ionian seaboard
it's practically a Seferis poem
until a plastic oar twangs in the air
& half the crew abandons ship
the water facilitated quick descending
light through clear green pulses
& waverings onto serrated limestone
craters cupping clutches of rounded stones
& thin fish with green & purple patterns
you couldn't tell from the surface how
you swam suddenly out over great
depths the water darkening like evening sky
& all forms become indistinct
hovering through evening light
at two in the afternoon
sun fierce on the blue
& unseen lines on my back

2.6 Monday 24th September

underground passages
unexpectedly complex
you can explore only so many
a lifetime isn't enough
as they say about Rome
Roma—non basta una vita
but some tunnels are dull
& there's the time you waste
prevaricating at junctions
the path you're on is your own
many of the passages
are low & narrow the water shallow
pebbles clear a foot below the surface
small lights illuminate the route
the boat rocks if we move
we duck our heads & proceed feeling
the roof recede beyond our reach
a breathtaking sensation
the world expands until a limestone spur
cuffs you on the shoulder as you snake
into the mountain the stone sky drips
slowly growing down to meet the ground
wherever it is rich enough
wherever it is rich enough
the ground rears up to meet it

2.7 Tuesday 25th September

a prickly pear grows in the first threshing floor
the second empty & overlooked
in a wild & fertile garden
an elderly woman dressed in black
pushes a wheelbarrow from the door
on the balcony
with its peeling blue railings
a man in his 60s demonstrates boxing moves
to an older man who sits & smiles & shakes his head
now we're inhabited by subterranean lakes
bigger than cities the sky reaches down
to kiss the surface anywhere anyone bothers to look
& so it is written or mentioned in passing
to a friend on the phone the methodology distilled
from everyone we've ever know especially those we
never met but read & it was more leaves to the tree
where still the sweet birds sing someone said
theory to poets is like ornithology to birds

3.1 Wednesday 26th September

this road passes more sacred spaces than you think
some holding their own remains in their arms
some disguised as shelters for pigs & goats
& this one where exhausted saints
point down to a child's plastic tractor
parked against the wall with candles
incense & a lighter
held in its half-raised bucket
further on & up is the monastery
a vast building site to its left
making the ground shake
then the beautiful small church
with its wonky cupola
the monastery is becoming abstract
very old olive trees all around
& one productive fig tree which feeds us
in the barren land up at the back
are spent shotgun cartridges
& two discarded pedaloes
the first pale lemon & upside down
with a rusty rectangular rudder
the other is tired blue over claret
& stands upright with chunky dignity
its pedals in excellent condition

3.2 Thursday 27th September

a dry tomato vine sprawls on the beach
just above the high-tide line & still growing
each ripe fruit salty & big as a pea
around the bright bay thin plots of land
lodged between the road & stone shacks
revert to a wildness
that endures for a few weeks
you garden the seasons for several years
using a similar hoe to your neighbours
cats slip through boundaries
dogs respond to barks from distant cousins
except for a few hunting dogs
which came from up in the mountains
or homes without obvious addresses
on the outskirts of the regional capital
now a rented bulldozer takes out
the tangled remains of a garden a century
or more in the making a vegetable plot slides
into the rocks at the top of the beach
the side gate still opens sweetly
but there's no fence left on either side
& then the gate goes onto the fire
bindweed decorates a rusted tap
some of the crops self-seeded leaving hints
of the shapes of the beds from years ago
the bulldozer nudges them over the edge
a couple of vegetable plants will self-seed
at the top of the beach in the lee of the road
for a few years to come & a cat will slide
through the new fencing past the new cars
parked on the new tarmac & disappear
into one of the small remaining patches
of greenery to begin a day

3.3 Friday 28th September

floating face down on the morning
sea I gaze blinking into Ionian silence
hiccough up the snorkel while a half-bubble
escapes from the corner of my mouth
easing its swaying way among sloping light
& shoals of finger-length fish turning left
because the world is turning like that today
people balancing on the hard bits
all feeling lonely together 'human being'
I don't like the multi-coloured hosepipe
fish poking out of that rock
it's one that can have your toes off
you can probably get rubber ones
you want to make the world more like how
the people you love secretly wish it to be
but sometimes you foreground the gap

3.4 Saturday 29th September

clothes line overspill waves from the trees
my blue T-shirt looks good on jasmine
your knickers wave hello & goodbye & other things
from the top of the bougainvillea
we hope they're not flicked into the sea
by more unexpected breezes we turn
our minds to decorating & rub our stomachs
we ate too much yoghurt so as to have somewhere
to clean the brushes in white spirits
at some point during the night a stranger
entered the square without disturbing the dogs
dropped some keys & left before dawn

3.5 Sunday 30th September

dawn at the end of September
the waning moon loosely moored
in the stirring eucalyptus tree
the constant unfolding of surf
muttering below the scent of jasmine
on which the night's last moths alight
brushing the flower which hardly moves
a touch like breath that's situated here
against the down on your forearm
& then is gone & it's lighter now
a little owl calls across chapel beach
as the light is turned off in the kitchen
four pine needles & their shadows on the rock
the dark nodding mid-morning sea
through the skin of the water
& deeper into another element
entering the ultramarine cave by touch
& in the still shadows of a sultry afternoon
honey slid glistening over figs

3.6 Tuesday 1st October

it's a new sun as long as we're moving
& it's rolled up over the mountain tops
by the process of standing on the ground
looking beyond the wall of the garden
there's something for everyone in the new
world supersite at a junction near you
not-for-profit provision of power
for light & heat & transport & communication
you can even have some water from the sky
without filling the pockets of shareholders
you can hear & say these words everywhere
TV radio oracle papers many heavens
the plates we left outside on the table
throughout the autumn nights are full of change

3.7 Tuesday 2nd October

it's a long way to the gates of Hades
you can get there via the Diros caves
please wear a hard hat
because the ancient people who lived here
stopped doing so
when an earthquake brought the roof down on their heads
& the roof was a mountain
this should have been the entrance to the underworld
& indeed it was
as is the place where each of us is standing
they used to rearrange their dead
into neat heaps until the big heap happened
& there was no-one left to rearrange them
until quite recently
thousands of mysterious points
shine down from the ceiling
there's always so much falling from the sky
her hands cupped in sleep

4.1 Wednesday 3rd October

this morning we pushed the boat out again
& all the flags disappeared
in the distance
the sea became bigger than perception
& there was scope for poetry once more
sometimes you need to move
away from houses with straight shadows
to a set of unfamiliar angles
& a restful kind of bracing sparseness
years are such small specks in the eye
they dump trailer-loads of muck out front
then the rusty wheelbarrow shrieks
the shovel & the cursing & the rake
bright evening rain sets in
the light fades
sky clears
away our traces overnight

4.2 Thursday 4th October

I paint the shoebox battleship grey
& drive past cave dwellings
now used as stores
& second homes for goats
Pan eyes behind the olive trees
until Kastania & the donkey
rocking up the Saidhona road
loaded with hearth sticks
it nodded & stopped next to Lynn
the owner had a big straw hat & asked
the donkey what it was doing
it looked up the slope then at Lynn
then at the owner & set off sighing
Kastania is wholly shaded by hills
all through the day & night it smells of trees
not leaves just the parts made of wood
the village is made of firewood
& stone & Lynn
winter always comes early
leaves late leading a donkey
without a tether
a basket in the yard

4.3 Friday 5th October

five small fishing boats rise & fall
along the harbour wall
a swallowed concertina of wave
I lob a bag of rubbish
in the communal bin & admire the effect
as three cats rocket out
in four different directions
the mountain top is as clean
& upstanding as a lizard
on a laptop case swallowing
as I reach for the wine
clicking on Ruby Braff's
What A Little Moonlight Will Do
he'd booked New York's Nola Studios
for 9/11 but they couldn't
start recording till the day after
with a modified line-up
as two of the players
couldn't get into
the devastated city
the reasons for not
making this music
are overwhelming

4.4 Saturday 6th October

a spinach pie in Diros
then the Serengheti
for Byzantine churches
new roads make old maps
more realistic
you just have to leave the car
& improvise your way along a line
leading nowhere except to this black pig
pottering outside a concrete bunker
piglets behind a green iron gate
go up & around & come back down
beyond the pigs to the dark green grove
which hides a terracotta glow
& space under piled stones
long straw-dry palm leaves
a cistern full of readiness & echoes
yawns beneath our feet
stays inside us
as we walk the line
drive further south
remembering the entrance
to the haunted cave
not much bigger
than your eye or ear
say the size of your heart or fist
to the the right
of the church door
an old bell hangs
from a tree
at hip height
new rope

4.5 Sunday 7th October

over Platsa
according to the book
another member of the Local Group
the galaxy M31
glows from two
million light years away
it's the sound of waves
rinsing rocks
autumn breathing in
& breathing out
Pegasus untethered
above the harbour
the creak of a damp rope
stretched tight
over the edges of peeling paint
& dry timber
as the small herd of boats
nods & grazes
& a fragment of bow
is left beached
in a circle of ash
on the shingle
the only thing left
is her name

4.6 Monday 8th October

they tied up the Temple of Apollo
in a canvas bag to keep the rain off
now it can't see over the vale
to the sea past the charred leaves
of Arcadia for miles
conceptual art in pewter
copper & matt black
the dark edges of the road
feathered with soot
& printed shadows flicked the way
the roaring wind of fire went
limping & sprinting
some of those caught
on the tinder slopes died
some were elsewhere
& lost everything
but their scorched hunger
& a sifting ache
for continuity that still
whispers the landscape
hurts most where local people
through dignity pride or modesty
had already pared things down
in their old age
which was swept away
in one the century's brightest nights
black empty tins on the lintel

4.7 Tuesday 9th October

black rusty shutters
clap in the breeze
new green growth
can be seen on the ground
by all those still here to see it
in places the fire
exploded in waves
roaring in every direction at once
stark photographs of the dark heart of light
developed as far as the mind could see
in the distance the legend of the beast
the petrol-soaked rag tied to a back leg
with electrical cable & then lit
so the fire seeds were sown in a mad plunge
zig-zagging through the world in an orgy
of fricatives & plosives
echoing around the desolate
cave of the mouth

5.1 Wednesday 10th October

pacing between the eyes
& the back of the head the poem's restless
even though that's where it's born
sleeps of a night & stashes its secrets
the view from the inside of the cave
up on the left is a dark ledge
the roof of the cave blackened by smoke
except for a swirl of grey
an intended sign
or the involuntary trace of a branch
being worked back into the opening
looking forwards there is the sea & sky
at a distance although looking forwards
is always also looking backwards here
the cave is as easy to defend
as it is to become trapped inside
Jesus a barn owl
that large pale wish made before you know it
a bird of strong omen
in an earlier incarnation
it tried to steal honey from the cave
in Crete where Zeus was born & resonates
honey was a metaphor & honey

5.2 Thursday 11th October

start with a stunning marble threshold
monsters blades & vines proclaim
a heady blend of opulence & power
carved in crystalline detail around the door
beyond a less impressive space
where working people looked at the bare floor
while straight-backed proprietors stalked past
with modest movements of their mouths & hands
a model of courtesy & restraint
one in a million one in a million
dressed in silk that falls straight to the ground
with the fluid grace of a poured fine wine
then there's a dark backyard of blood-marked earth
where feral cats kill with economy

5.3 Friday 12th October

eagle level with the mountain top
drift on another invisible wave
over pink bows along a balcony
celebrating a wedding or the birth
of someone who's pink there's another
click in the courtyard that's the third beetle
today I've turned up the right way
they wait a minute checking all their legs
& shields are on right then they trundle off
in a straight line with a sturdy
absence of indecision straight into
a thick limestone wall off they go again
in apparently random directions
I think we can learn a lot from beetles
but I don't know what
they seem to say
if you've got six legs use them
& we haven't even got onto wings

5.4 Saturday 13th October

we lost the path
so scrambled over sharp rocks & thorn
to the headland's tip
where we don't fall into
the intensely blue sea
no-one else on Tigani
some stone enclosures
have locked gates
& rudimentary roofs
most of the salt pans are disappearing
like the castle with its columns
lintels gaps & cisterns
& butterflies hard at work in the air
it's good to drink water
& walk on stone
making our way to the pirate village
crumbling around the cats
who leer & look sideways away
from their hoards

5.5 Sunday 14th October

at the end of the harbour path
the sun fell into three feet of green water
a kingfisher flicked out of the shadows
& flew low out towards the horizon
the steel ladder bolted to the rock
led down into deeper & darker water
the bed of irregular boat-shearing
limestone formed sharp-edged cauldrons
lined with smooth white egg pebbles
glistening with quartz &
a treasury of breath & centuries
after a tin of squid & a mouthful
of Metaxas Taurus enters the field
of night & rests its head on the gate

5.6 Monday 15th October

a car came by every evening
loudspeaker clamped to the roof
shouting about a politician
& how we'd go forwards together
forever starting with the forthcoming
but the car had already passed by
accelerating to the next village
I carry on cooking sausage pasta
with Greek bangers & a very curly
chilli pepper when the same car
comes racing back past the chapel as if
something important had been forgotten
this time the car's going slightly faster
& disappears without a word

5.7 Tuesday 16th October

there's more air in the mountains but less room
for the sky what with all this pointed rock
here's where she laughed & said it looks as if
that mountain is hugging the other one
you do a course then fill a plastic tray
stir in the western saffron streak of pain
with rice & molasses & the tender
flakes of fish you swam with
this morning sheer poetry isn't just
this silver in the keep-net
at dusk you're in for the long haul feeling
you'll never see the nets drawn in
rising into a chilling night sky
opening over the cavernous hold

6.1 Wednesday 17th October

scraps of rubbish
flattened in the surface of the earth
plastic bottle tops fruit rind
cabbage stalks discarded pages
lids of margarine tubs
& the stink of feral cat
at the bottom of the cliff
on a patch of weeds & pebbles
a soft nest of rusty flakes
used to be a dustbin
it's good to start from scratch
& it's good to improvise on old tunes too
the sun eases itself over the mountain
after breakfast this morning
in no hurry & with little warmth
this may take some time the sun says
go & do something lively
hang your rugs over the gate
smack the dust back out
buy coffee & brandy & vegetables
later we'll talk about autumn

6.2 Thursday 18th October

some weeks last months
you slipped off the red dress
in the twinkling of two eyes
we walked the deserted city
through the fragile summer night
with light purposeful steps
& no idea of where to go
a completion of autumn sunshine
settles through the gaps
of the garden behind the house
where if you close your eyes
you see trumpets & watercress
paintbrushes & brandy
a small stone dish of salt
skin under very thin clothing
& the mistakes
like cactus-flavoured ice-cream
refusing to melt in the gutter
but here's a butterfly
with shapely lemon wings
& at the tip of each
soft orange patches
clapping together noiselessly
over your flowers

6.3 Friday 19th October

to reach Milia by car
says the map
turn right at Stoupa
drive through Pirgos
past the goats on the left who are still in bed
& the cows on your right who are not there
the sun goes unexpectedly behind
a scrap of cloud no bigger than your hand
held at the end of your arm in the sky
fast approaching the Milia junction
here we should turn right but go straight on
to Kastania because we like it
stop at the first church
St John's where a padlock is padlocked to
a padlock from which an old bit
of wire snares a nail in the door
lift the wire & go in admiring the way
your mass alters the shape of the space inside
with its small choirs of interlocking curves
& the dusty grey light
that whispers down to touch you

6.4 Saturday 20th October

we go on haunting the places we love
coming in from yet another angle
walking up the track to skirt the village
surprising the mad cat in the bin
who scratches wailing
at the sloping sides of the hollow box
then zooms out splayed against
the air with the plastic that held a
4-pack of beer round one leg
& a lolly wrapper on its ear
that is not a healthy diet
overshoot the village so you see it
well disposed below with its cats & dogs
craning their necks & tails at the humans
clambering down past vegetable terraces
to Agios Petros & its tower
in here it is best not to walk backwards
from the paintings into the dangling lamp
which flickers & sips holy oil
because it may tip all over your shirt
& not wash out even with Greek Omo

6.5 Sunday 21st October

we go up & left & right & back down
& then in some more directions
to retrieve the church of St Nicholas
the old ladies have straw hats the same width
as the alleys our heads are the same height
as the feet of two sitting to the north
they stare expressionless
as going around the steep little block
we lose sight of them but then re-emerge
with our eyes level with their waists right here
good morning we say
where have you been? they ask
& where are you going?
to St Nicholas we say
where is St Nicholas today?
an old lady with a straw hat so wide
the pale edges flap like wings as she moves
picks up a giant tub of tile grouting
& beckons us to follow
up left right along right left down up
right left along right
about four feet as the crow flies
there
there he is
thank you very much goodbye
St Nick—be with you
go towards the good
there are no directions

6.6 Monday 22nd October

lift up the stick that stops the door
swinging open in the breeze & enter
this fine space full of dark icons
& folding chairs building materials
& acres of fresh-faced paintings
that long red tongue down which you slip
straight through the throat of hell
the see-through sack of souls being carted
across the west wall away from the lion
camels deer & artist's private bestiary
the fish with an arm thrust
out of its mouth one with a leg
one with a person's head
Nick bigger than the boat in which he floats
Prince Charles with big wings where his ears should be
the last judgement tuning up with angels
on horns in the ultimate brass section
signs of the zodiac singing the songs
we hummed on the way back down the mountain
where a donkey accelerated past
tail ears & salutation rushing by
as it stood up in the back of an old
pick-up truck leaning into the corners

6.7 Tuesday 23rd October

I was going to read this afternoon
but I don't really feel like reading
I feel like watching this
stunning black bee
with iridescent electric-blue wings
under the threatening slate clouds
treading & kneading the shining white
bougainvillea flowers
each with its firm perky trumpets
which poke the bee when it starts
stirring & cycling with its skinny
strong back legs
I don't want to read when the bee leans
heavily off into the darkening sky
we walk the coast road in the rain
luminous silver gaps in the cloud

7.1 Wednesday 24th October

wriggling through a gap in Kalamata
through to the startling Sparta road
driving higher & thinner & tighter through passes
a rare cold precipice drops you breathing
& closing the window on vertigo
& ash from burned out sheds & tavernas
the ghost of a weighing scale hangs above
a blackened table as we park in a cloud
the windscreen wipers smearing damp red dust
in seeping arcs to show a rectangle
of charcoal on the ground beside the road
a bent metal sign whispers Honey
in grey ghosts of Greek & English script
where impenetrable thorn cover grew
a hunter steps through black calligraphy

7.2 Thursday 25th October

empty dwellings haunt cavernous clearings
through charred glades by the side of the road
still smelling of smoke & smouldering tyres
the roadside shrine that whistled in the fire
sheds little scabs of paint with autumn leaves
where trunks & branches have been cleared away
from the road & verges using chain saws
you see the fire has left the thinnest of black rings
around an untouched core of perfect wood
we watch the sky raining over Mystras
an important outpost of Narnia
& stop for petrol in Magoula where there's
a toilet just past the inspection pit
then left through the grey metal doors
you can buy any make of car in Sparta

7.3 Friday 26th October

we pulled in to photograph the mountains
too near an army base full of Spartans
having a fag in camouflage jackets
rattling down the Evrotas valley
we admire the productive greenery
& the range of cement mixers for sale
in builders' merchant every half mile
while checking the rear-view mirror
& spotting the biggest stockpile of bricks
outside China the rain stopped in Githio
we reversed up a steep back street to park
then walked down & across to the island
the site of Paris & Helen's first night
surrounded by small fish & a duck club
there's a scruffy wood a boatyard full of wrecks
a lighthouse & a man fishing near his car
a Mercedes parked blocking the footpath
by the sign saying no cars or campers
we finished the figs & invested in
half a kilo of goat bells & a mop

7.4 Saturday 27th October

I dream in a chair made of canvas & wood
on a terrace with lemons & basil
above the noise of inner-city traffic
& I have no idea of where I am
& I have no idea of who I am
except clotted scents & a wisp of air-brakes
the jab of a church spire sharp through the gaps
in a soap opera from somewhere down below
I know the light is becoming thinner
& I should have called someone by now
maybe my wife or my son or daughter
my parents or an editor back home
the first stars emerge in a mid-green sky
somebody knocking at a distant door

7.5 Sunday 28th October

a church high above the Ionian
as the first windless day for a week ends
in a wide stillness in which sounds emerge
lapping this ledge: a woman talking to
a neighbour hundreds of feet below
a gun dog chained to a rusting tractor
barks with a hoarse & mournful hoot
a lizard flicks through a crack in the locked church
three different sheep bells neither harmonise
nor clash but inhabit the darker sound
of the sea far below which almost gasps
almost continuously & so it should
carrying for miles & years through the scrub
of this old basket of litter & stars

7.6 Monday 29th October

not much sleep up early not much food
eat yoghurt on toast for breakfast & throw
things we didn't know we had in the skip
ducking to avoid ejector-seat cats
drive south before dawn to Areopoli
to head north on the Githion road
& onwards up to the mountain village
where the road momentarily vanished
in a cold high square & an old woman
selling chestnuts in blue carrier bags
moved around the square bent almost double
by age & aches & her absence of weight
we spotted the road & drove north again
on a glorious switchback through limestone
cliffs & trees coloured by autumn & fire
more bare deserted charcoal tables perched
by black diagrams of woodland showing
it's too late for a while for honey
we descend to wide dried-up river valleys
& on to meet the spirit of renewal
near the oil depot in Elefsina

7.7 Tuesday 30th October

I got the mosquito with an orange
then I ate the orange: justice is done
in airports the blues is turned to trifle
& because travel makes you really thick
why not buy four kilos of Toblerone
& a bottle of Scotch for eighty quid
the engines start up so do the babies
howling over the lights of Piraeus
then we & the babies are swept up to
twenty-six thousand feet over somewhere
too much like Switzerland for its own good
above the earth in the dark thoughts turn
to Norfolk winter saltmarsh & footpaths
meeting at the edge of Brancaster woods
where colonies of snails roost in the trees
mid-evening over a place like France &
from this height the world is decorated
by humanity with gold & silver
lights of habitation embroidered over
the rich dark cloak of earth with moonlight
flowing down our rivers past the churches
schools & hospital blocks to the lighthouse
poised by the shimmering acres of sea
I foolishly thought that writing this poem
would make me happier & it did

Physical Geography

Rocks

it's hard to recognise
the shift of virtual plates
inside the mind
the catastrophes stick
the scalding eruptions
& seismic kicks
that leave you for weeks
without skin
this month
the business is more everyday
a cheque to the plasterer
the performance management cycle
a gas meter reading
taking the old computer to the tip
consulting the oracle
of a forgotten god near Islip
these shoes won't do
dig out the boots from the loft
for the first time in seven years
strike camp with sun singing
the hand is made of so many issues
which believe themselves unique
& at the centre of the universe
in this case are the muscovite
the felspars & the quartz
over on your right
are the ferromagnesian group
such as olivine hornblende & biotite
behind you are the chlorides sulphides
iron oxides & carbonates
consider the range of density & lustre
colour hardness cleavage & history

they haven't always been this cold
in these regions
inhabitants congregate
for key dates of the calendar
saying: let's unpack the instruments
& knock out some atonal music
the outer surfaces
contain unexpected pressures
when these are locally relieved
the interior shifts
& something moves towards the surface
along lines of weakness or desire
energies settle in varied ways
silica everywhere you look
acid rock tends to be lighter
with a more pronounced bass
magmatic differentiation
generates barely visible
crystal ladders
if magma cools in great deep pools
it does so slowly
forming plutonic rocks
with large crystals
some larger than your garden
some igneous rocks crack as they cool
studies of exposed sections of the mind
show pentagonal or hexagonal columns
soaring up & downwards to the future
chemical & physical disintegration
precedes temporary reunification
in modified locations through
diagenesis or affection

aspects of the past form clastic planks
you cannot hold in your hands
but may glide or slip upon
in certain atmospheric conditions
metamorphic processes transformed us
into next days that look into the wind & blink
then we stooped at either end of the garden
to ease perfectly good weeds into the breeze
I thought
if it hadn't come by May
it wouldn't come at all
three or four years passed
& I stopped looking
at that vacant space
between the garden & the sea
it was 7 years later
as I stood at dusk facing south
hands dumped in my pockets
that the angel
called the song of the earth
turned & glanced this way
I walked through
the meteorite storm
inside my head
I stood upon the patch
of barren ground
where lightning
whipped & smouldered
it felt like changing colour
from the feet up
the scale of outcrop
depends on dip

Millstone Grit
retired from racing years ago
Oxford clay shelly & oolitic limestones chalk marls
nodules of chert all dragged by sluggish troughs of ice
across the base of my lake
lignite
Marmite
natural gas
                        Durham Dolomite

Dead Sea alabaster   the bed sheets bent westwards

                        Swedish magnetites

Bohemian metamorphics   Belgian slates

Welsh schist   movement under the groundsheet
                            angular unconformity
countless varves
dendrochronological cartoon characters
going round in circles
some rocks bathe in the rain
others swallow streams
without so much as blinking
all rock is haunted by run off & spring
most rock resents a boggy hollow
all the coals
a range of slates
the bones of roads
cement
cement & plaster
brick gravel sand

stone for milling & grinding
whetstones
salt
phosphates   potash
metal ore
silver zinc & lead   tin & manganese
copper   iron
platinum   & gold
sensual erosion of graphite

Air

I'm not going to say much
more than *aria / contretemps*
ear connected to the back of the throat
raw from stains in the air
the stares   stars   stores
each only as full as a window
the little heard
pattering behind you
on the night leaves
all the voices in the air
& head choir of living
& dying with angels
benign aspirations suppressed
by conventional signs
money & hand signals
we wanted a little
local transfiguration
but popped to the toilet
30 seconds before
what could've been
a crucial moment
now it's raining in the wind
the new dog has a freckled velvet
snout you don't mind
the hole in your bucket
if your bucket's full
of coal I'm not going to say
much more than aria I
beg to disagree there's a stairway
made of breath
that moves up past
fundamental numbers

it climbs the light at night
& follows subtle changes of
key familiar & local
there's more wine under the
stairs than you think it
doesn't have to be flamenco
breakfast in trousers is fine
we'll empty the ash when
it's worth emptying the ash
when we can no longer
start the fire you
can't tell the story until
the story's done
as you twang its strands
allowing air into deadly
affiliations get your beans in
to the only weeded patch
sometimes there's only time
to weed & plant simultaneously
with deft flicks of the wrist
thousands of initiates
could chant these words
wearing golden robes
driving on remoulds
wearing air that passes by
like a clear contemporary
who moves into advertising
wearing air you can see
through the deterioration
of your eyes all the way
to the construction site
whistling both ways

through these weeds
teeth & trees you have only
this one chance again
& again to seethe with
ignorance & knowledge
riding & being ridden by
this glimpse of that's all
do it now & help
turn in the draft

Lakes

no sooner do you see them
than they're gone
some duck behind bushes
some are too loved up
by the sun
a few had their grants cut
& one took offence
because we described
its attributes as laky
instead of lacustrine
some duck behind bushes
cackles rudely then
does a headstand in it
even big ones are sensitive
they look in each direction
simultaneously
& feel their highest water
kissed away by breezes
& straight-faced promises
yet their own sins glower
beneath & accumulate
lakes are unsure of their edges
& where their next drink's
coming from
they prefer anglers
to composers & poets
who misrepresent them
they feel that remote corners
they've lost touch with
are seeping life-blood into
bottomless rock & powder
they are surprised

that you can hold one
in the palm of your hand

Coastlines

the spaces in between your fingers
shift throughout the day
& almost disappear in sleep
when everything merges into the imagined
it's easy to underestimate
the extent to which the land goes up & down
before you even reach the coast
the sea goes to work   then it goes home
the job description changes
as do the work stations
new equipment & services
minimising health & safety
here comes the send   the swash
which turns inside out   falling
through itself as backwash
arranging funerals for your toes
pretending not to care as you stare
far beyond fictional alternatives
the gasp & pluck of lives unlived
the sea can turn us into babies
waves draw circles in the sea with water
which washes them away
yet I think it's how the mind began
& begins to surround the idea of the sea
undertow is the most haunting
side of wave action
notwithstanding the scale
of oceanic fetch
& land rising behind
vertiginous   cadences ringing
down inside yourselves for good
comprising piles of loose recycled land

carted away by undistinguished trickles
or dissolved like luminous sweets
in the mouths of children   lost & forgotten
promises made a few miles inland
within the weatherproof walls of houses
at night the sea is more visible
without its camouflage of sky & light
it is mostly made of interiors
inside more interiors   disposed in long
deconsecrated vaults through which
the trappings of the living & the dead
as well as those caught in between
drift down the unfathomable
& decreasingly green
fathoms turning at awkward angles
disenfranchised satellites
plunging invisibly downwards
panels already rusting
caving in to dark pressure
it's all so different from celery
for example

Deserts

deserts do not last for long
as they have no roofs
they are reconfigured
by lunatic waters
when no-one is looking
then their edges
are cooked & frozen
into hoover-bag dust
for disassembly
by the winds
they occupy the tropical
west of continents
& high mid-continental shelves
marooned in the rain-shadows
of neighbouring mountains
& zones of postponed aspiration
you take the A10 south as far as Spain
you're moving there even though you're not
then S.E. from Marrakech or Shepherd's Bush
past troops heading back the other way
when you reach the middle of the desert
you see the sweet green fields of long ago
that never actually existed
you need to pace out the perimeter
of your future settlement with the real
where the only water comes in on our backs
every time we think we're up to date
this hair grows back across our limbs & faces
I lost my whistle & cadastral maps
I stubbed my head on the wall
& thought the door was on the other side
Billy Smith showed me A minor

on his sister's birthday
the cider was bright
& bigger than your stomach
he said he reckoned
I could finger his sister
I didn't know what that meant
in the film the guy said
they fingered me for something I didn't do
the road had seen no rain in weeks
she sang at the Gray Dawn in Queens
when she was maybe 16 or 17
it rained just as hard in Baltimore
let's get one thing clear
it's not the job of poetry
to add sand or borders to the world
past the plastic tunnels of southern Spain
where minimum wage
involves sips of water & untethered dogs
we look across the straits
this account of deserts
is quivering with truth & objectivity
deserts gradually develop
then they go away
some are formed before your birth
& leave long after you're gone
so you do need to think about address
& the history of aesthetics
as the context of your art
as a rare evening rain
drifts though the sun
I'm glad the old red sandstone is buried
with our pips   egg shells   sticky love

our sense that deserts are just
one of the settings for wrong
turning after turning in after turning

Glaciation

ice shaped this land
by scraping   or fridge-defrost
run-off with insufficient J-cloths
or smearing foreign gardens
across your path
it altered the shape of your nose
the extent of your shade
the depth of your vegetable patch
the water of the world
calls the water we are made of
which never was quite the same thing
a retired glacier insinuates itself
into your innerness
whispering down your neck
throat & into your ears—
it'll trickle down your spine
congeal in the small of your back
then one evening
it starts to harden   turning from blood
to fat to muscle to cold bony fists
that drag your face off
on the landscape of your habits:
sacred configurations gorgeous knolls
spiritually-charged cairns
dainty counterfeit molehills
profound gorges made by gods
your grandad liked
who trundled south from heaven
on the last of a long line of white elephants
down the Alpine valleys
all the way to Norwich
glaciation puts colour in your cheeks

normally blue & green
exfoliates the fringes of complexion
then buffs your nails   then nails
your butt to terminal moraine
snow can be sung away
by warm birds in spring
or form deadening layers
through extra compaction
snow may melt by day
but then percolate deeper in
& refreeze even closer to your heart
in a form of sublimation
the diverse layers of the firn field
the earlier falls & deposits
metamorphosed into gristle & armour
in which it's hard to dance
though your planted ski-stick
picks up catchy frequencies
the density of new snow (0.1)
the density of the hardest glacier ice (over 0.9)
the density of your next thought
yet glaciers can move faster than you think
the middle moves faster than the sides
& as the slope gets less steep
the front of the glacier slows
while the higher speed behind
results in awkward thickening
the complexities of direction & flow
see the lines forming in the perceptors
ice pressure may result in a layer of water
between the glacier & the ground
glacial systems often breach preglacial

watersheds & creosoted fences
the gap between the back of the glacier
& the rock wall of its basin
is called a bergschrund
& should be treated with respect
even though there's nothing there
much is written on the layers
& cracks within along & across
glaciers & aspects of your bodywork
some are clear as skin in adverts
some are rough & bubbly with
dirt bands seasonal shifts tyre marks
Januaries twelve weeks long
numb summers   carbon emissaries
high-heeled tourists ideological troughs
& memories of glaciers singing badly
easily mistaken for whales
singing to pregnant pauses
in expensive local clinics
because of all the marine creatures
found in amniotic fluid these days
moraines are badly constructed earthworks
slapped up by French peasants on Fridays
then blamed on distant glints
glacierets come in a range of sizes
you can put some in your drink
glaciers shrink then disappear
as supply is exceeded by wastage
when the base of a glacier freezes
onto rock then moves forwards
exaration occurs (balls pulled off)
then scouring   brilloing

deep cleansing   effective removal of the surface
wave to the sky behind the feeling
see the lines farming in the perceptors
reflect in the nivation hollow
melt-water seeps down
your bergschrund & randkluft
your eyeball connected to your root-ball
endless swivelling bedding in
wearing out wearing in
bedding out   lubrication
preventing the devastation
when we all do our own thing
we get the pyramidal peak of the Matterhorn:
the firn field nestles in its bowl
wiggles in with time & irritation
you're here to stay
below a certain temperature
completely unaware of head-wall recession
that leaves you back to back
with someone shielding a smoking gun
or maybe breathing out knife-edge arêtes
even after all these years
the birds that flew above you
never show up on the records
stoss-&-lee   crag-&-tail
the doorways ranged along the royal mile
a polar bear drives a white Princess
in areas of knob & lochan relief
you can play giants & rock pools
urstromtäler   phantom valleys
glaciation can deliver other
people's landscapes to your neighbourhood

with rocks as big as vans inside the ice
rock flour sand & shingle squirt along
in melt-water currents on or through or under
ice like vital memories or diseases
anticipations of a whole new world
all mashed & stirred by what we breathe
into the darkness   the older drifts
while we wait for the younger drifts
just under your skin are the erratics
the perched blocks   till & hoover bags
an erratic may contain a quarry
be gnawed into the form of a village
& like the shards in your head
will contain connate water
trapped way back in geological time
though constantly pierced & stirred
by every wave & particle under the sun
you could live for years on one moraine
the Cromer ridge   14 miles long   5 wide
what used to be bulges
now little pits & pingos
many features are time-transgressive
once hereabouts it was sub-Arctic
& now the ice is retreating
even from its heartlands
the lorries go by
with a new generation of fridges
all set to work hard to earn their keep
the white blossom on the small tree
at the bottom of the garden
has been there only a week
but already the petals fall

through very still air
each time the bee touches the flower

Underground Water

it's coming on Christmas
they're cutting down trees
the river's been dragged
down to Hades once more
through an expressionless
swallow-hole I wish I had
a river to skate away on
towards the first Ely house lights
you can get holy water
in large plastic containers
with moulded handles
as used by caravanners
who waddle back from taps in fields
with grim lop-sidedness
to help anchor their flimsy
structures during gales
or trial by motorway slipstream
it's important to remember
that much of the land
is invisible to water
which therefore lands
beneath it
in secret venues
meteoric water
is involved in the traditional
physical assumption
then reincarnation rigmarole
enjoyed by teachers
many rocks let water
through their very being
others are just riddled with cracks
in certain caverns

you may glimpse a pale creature
with large eyes obsessively
muttering about which path
it arrived down
from the white stones
these are lost Cambridge poets
& it is customary to pretend
they are not there
some water has never
seen the light of day
in recent aeons at least
& is connate water
subterranean activity
may free it from its tomb
then it is known as juvenile water
oceanic water has seeped
inland from seas
& has hardly started
Artesian basins
remind you why your fingers
don't grow directly
from your shoulders
the main Cambridge aquifer
is Lower Greensand
sandwiched between months of clay
an oasis is where the sky
has swept all the paraphernalia
from the water table
it is best not to confuse
water table with water bed
or Walter Mitty
who was Keats' lover

in his head
Simon Fell is surrounded
by sink-holes
conflict may occur
between different interest groups
in a cavern system
there are separate zones
for activities involving incantation
pickled eggs & sexual liaison
although on off-season weekdays
you may pursue all three & more
under the one roof
& in the selfsame niche
if you have a torch
sturdy footwear & have not
left clear indications
of your plans with a badge
in certain Pennine caves
pickles have been found
dating back to the Bronze Age
caves are good for smugglers
bats pirates & old testamental
fundamentalists such as
Mr Bin Laden who may be
inhabiting one of the 50,000
sink-holes gracing the Kentucky
plateau thousands of miles
from civilization
dry valleys are enjoyed by sheep
& children rolling sideways
they were formed
like everything else

under conditions which
no longer exist
except for overweight parent
helpers on school trips who do
other causes of dry valleys
are transformed water tables
exploding water beds
the temporary impermeability
of permafrost
spring-sapping
& enormous dragons
the devil had nothing to do
with dry valley formation
in spite of the names of many
some collapsed caverns
turn into gorges
which may be colonized
by the National Trust
or elves & old fridges
under exceptional
geomorphological conditions
gorges may rise
in any case it is wise
to scatter your ashes
in a gorge before you are dead
& although caves
get many squinting
for the altar
you must resist
for the sake of your eyes
& the world
just sing a rousing shanty

in your head
with made-up names
of prehistoric nymphs
bring along some reading material
as a reminder of Pan
& of the city
such as Stephen Rodefer
or Walter Raleigh
the words will see you
home before dark
to feed & water your head
supporting it at window height
above the well-stacked dead
recycling the passion
your rising damp
your saturated vault
that chemical dye
squirted in your heart
at birth shows the course
of your journey to
the end

Vulcanicity

turmoil case flexing crisp shells leather
most of the noises stay out of earshot
the gases swap colours in the darkness
chest pains may come & go throughout the day
but perch on the head of the bed all night
most of us come from vulcanicity
it kisses the skin from our fingertips
it keeps the edges of thought free of frost
dykes can keep rabbits out of your garden
while sills hover above the town for miles
leaden lids buried in builders' rubble
a resting place for sheep & north-east winds
batholiths are satellites & planets
that never managed to complete their birth
& remain as monumental tombstones
in memory of a world that's still to come
not everything is better out than in
scorching jets of toxins cook the rabbit
weld the only hand tools to a tractor
torch the hall in an unwitnessed ritual
bomb the goats with pyroclasts & gravy
drive hot-rods into the city sideways
a visit by the package-deal from hell
leaves the meadows simmering for a month
lava flow like so much else depends on
how much silica & gas is in there
when you retire you can start to go brown
but why wait till the floods arrive to start
caravanning with Nietzsche—before long
they'll announce the discovery of dark
matter inside the mind
the last noise you hear

Rivers

after immeasurably
short distances downstream
you can't tell which is
the oldest water in the river
the tributaries rain &
seepage are all lost
in the sense of found
as the river approaches its name
headstreams sometimes merge
or at least run briefly parallel
but many strike out in
opposite directions
even though they start
a spit apart
rivers wear away
carry & let slip
their odour changes like your own
it's rarely home cooking
the water changes & makes
& changes the land
America is being lowered
a yard every 30,000 years
by every style of surface water
but it is also being raised
by other kinds of bullshit
some of which are known as
isostatic compensation
eventually everywhere
becomes a peneplain
which is like a level
playing field only bumpy
& level only in theoretical models

but never seen
except in certain
Hampshire camp sites
steepness varies alarmingly
& rejuvenation may occur
at any time
depending on where
the monkey-gland man
torches his van
polycyclic relief
is the shape of
everyone's profile
who has ever
dipped a finger
into water
I knew an interfluve
who could stand up
for no more than two hours
at a time
I now know this is true
of everyone
except certain sentries
who are mainly Hirst installations
which distract attention
from the purpose
of the building in the background
it is important
not to irritate academics
when you talk
or write about rivers
& the water heading that way
covers all the land

it patters into heather
& on rock
& sheep & your cagoule
the bus shelter
Mazdas & corgis
snug blazers
loose hoods
loose molls & wardens
bridges   piazzas
railway tracks
service stations   buds
tree branches
fallen leaves
extensions   sheds
outhouses   pubs
water butts
well-rotted organic
matter in allotments
municipal borders
ferry terminals
ponds   runways
playgrounds
umbrellas
sports fields
building sites
window boxes
graves
on its way
to the river
before tethering your goat
for extended periods
like that long weekend

in Barcelona
from November to March
or before attaching
a mill wheel
to your caravan
check seasonal variations
in the flow of your river
& while a spring
may seem delightfully
straightforward
bear in mind
springs slowly
eviscerate
their site & eat
backwards into bone

Printed in the United Kingdom by
Lightning Source UK Ltd., Milton Keynes
141049UK00001B/30/P